Give God the Glory!
Let Your **Light** So Shine!

By

Kevin Wayne Johnson

1

Give God the Glory! Let Your Light So Shine, a devotional

Note: This book was originally published in 2004 by Tate
Publishing, Mustang, OK, and Writing for the Lord Ministries,
Hillsborough, NJ, under a different ISBN. The new ISBN (below)
reflects the most recent publication by Writing for the Lord
Ministries, Clarksville, MD.

Distributed throughout the United States of America, Canada,
Europe, Australia and South America by:

Advocate Distribution Services
a division of Send the Light Distributors
100 Biblica Way
Elizabethton, TN   37643 (USA)
(423) 547-5100 phone
(423) 547-5199 fax
www.stl-distribution.comPlus eleven (11) other global strategic
distribution partners (as listed at www.writingforthelord.com)

ISBN: 978-0-9883038-0-5

LCCN: 2012951660

Printed in the United States of America by:

Lightning Source, Incorporated, a division of INGRAM BOOKS
1246 Heil Quaker Boulevard
LaVerge, Tennessee   37086
www.lightningsource.com

Light defines the very essence of the children of God. It is a word that is used throughout The Holy Bible 264 times! It is characterized as an element that:
Illuminates
Shines
Exposes and expels darkness
Projects and extends brightness
Causes one to see
Radiates, and
Reveals.

Light, phos, derives from roots pha-and phan-in the original Greek language. In this context, man is naturally incapable of receiving spiritual light inasmuch as he lacks the capacity for spiritual things. Once converted through the saving knowledge of Jesus Christ, believers are called 'sons of light' not merely because we have received a revelation from God, but because in the New Birth, we have received the spiritual capacity for it.

Through our light, we make God visible to all men and demonstrate that His love transcends all that is wrong with this world. Now, let's **Give God the Glory!**

1.

Let Your Light Shine

You are light; You are the express
image of God and are made
in **His** likeness.

(Genesis 1:26)

Contents

"Ye are the light of the world.   A city that is set on an hill cannot be hid."

(Matthew 5:14)

＿＿＾◦◦＾＿＿

You are a visible and integral part of God's plan to reconcile others to Christ. Through you–your lifestyle, mannerism, and uniqueness–others will know that there is a true and living God.
You are on display.

"Let your light so shine before men, that they may see
your good works, and glorify your Father
which is in heaven."

(Matthew 5:16)

Be a visible manifestation of the Heavenly Father
through your kind attitude, ethical behavior,
unwavering patience, and uncompromising integrity.
To this end, God is glorified through you–
His willing earthen vessel.

"As long as I am in the world, I am the light of the world."
(John 9:5)

Jesus Christ is the light of the world.
Through salvation, you now live, move, and have
your being in Christ. Thus, His light resides
within you.

"For we were sometimes darkness, but now are ye light in the Lord: walk as children of light."

(Ephesians 5:8)

Unfulfillment and discontent were prevalent in our daily walk before Jesus Christ came into our lives. Through His grace and mercy, enjoy the spiritual tra nsformation and walk in the newness of life. Walk as children of the light through spiritual awareness and right living so that others will desire to know that Jesus is Lord.

"For so hath the Lord commanded us, saying, 'I HAVE SET THEE TO BE A LIGHT OF THE GENTILES, THAT THOU SHOULDEST BE FOR SALVATION UNTO THE ENDS OF THE EARTH.'"

(Acts 13:47)

The Apostle Paul revealed his light to the Gentiles during his sermon on the second Sabbath. Having been rejected by the Jews, his salvation message was received gladly by the Gentiles. In turn, they became light throughout the region of Asia Minor, publishing the Word of the Lord.

"While ye have light, believe in the light, that ye may be the children of light. These things spake Jesus, and departed, and did hide himself from them."

(John 12:36)

Be convinced that you are light in the midst of this dark world. Believe it, through faith, so that our Heavenly Father can use you to make a difference!

2.

Light as an Extension of Brightness

Our Heavenly Father shows you the way.   In all of your ways, acknowledge Him, and He shall direct your paths.

(Proverbs 3:6)

"The LORD is my light and my salvation; whom shall I fear? The LORD is the strength of my life; of whom shall I be afraid?"
(Psalm 27:1)

⟡

Light is a characteristic of God. Trust in the Lord and do not be afraid of the opposition directed toward you while you are sharing the gospel of Jesus Christ.

"And I will bring the blind by a way that they knew
not; I will lead them in paths that they have not known:
I will make darkness light before them, and the crooked
things straight. These things will I do unto them,
and not forsake them."

(Isaiah 42:16)

Take comfort in God's Word.   God will lead, guide, and
direct you in every area of your life. He will light your
path, provide simple–yet clear–instructions, and offer
clear guidance in your daily walk.

"And unto his son will I give one tribe,
that David my servant may have a light always
before me in Jerusalem, the city which I have
chosen me to put my name there."

(1 Kings 11:36)

God can, and will, use you to light the way as you fulfill your predestined assignment in the earth. He has a plan for your life. In due season, He will exalt you as others do not respond to their divine calling. God needs you to trust and obey.

"Light is sown for the righteous, and gladness for the upright in heart."

(Psalm 97:11)

Rejoice in the Lord! This anthem of praise reveals that light is reserved for the righteous. With clean hands and a pure heart, let your light be a demonstration to others that Jesus is Lord!

"Thou shalt also decree a thing, and it shall
be established unto thee: and the light shall shine
upon thy ways."

(Job 22:28)

Eliphaz, the Temanite, whose name means 'God for
strength,' debated with Job three times during Job's six
months of suffering.   His encouraging words convinced
his friend Job to trust in the Lord, pray, and seek His face.
When He answers the prayer, His light shall shine upon
him. Encourage a friend today.

"The entrance of thy words giveth light; it giveth understanding unto the simple."

(Psalm 119:130)

Be open to receive God's Word.   By allowing yourself to learn, the revelation and understanding of His Word will overtake you. It will transcend your educational level and pierce your inner man. Your heart and mind will be renewed through spiritual knowledge and kingdom principles. Then, your words will be light–illuminating–as you spread the gospel.

19

"Rejoice not against me, O mine enemy: when I fall,
I shall arise; when I sit in darkness, the LORD
shall be a light unto me."

(Micah 7:8)

This prophet of God holds out the hope of restoration to
the rich and influential people of Jerusalem. As the rich
mistreat the poor, and as the kingdom of Israel continues to
crumble inwardly and outwardly until its actual collapse,
Micah acknowledges the promise of salvation. He knows,
and confesses, that even in the midst of evil, the light of the
Lord will shine upon him.

"That was the true Light, which lighteth every man that cometh into the world."

(John 1:9)

Jesus Christ is the light of the world. Through Him, we come to know and understand that God's revelation is universally available. Its characteristics are beauty, radiance and utility.   It represents all that is radiant and luminous in the mental, moral, and spiritual life of men and angels. Acceptance of Jesus Christ gives us the ability to know God's plan for our lives.

21

"This then is the message which we have heard of Him, and declare unto you, that God is light, and in Him is no darkness at all. If we say that we have fellowship with Him, and walk in darkness, we lie, and do not the truth: But if we walk in the light, as He is in the light, we have fellowship one with another, and the blood of Jesus Christ His Son cleanseth us from all sin."

(1 John 1:5-7)

God is perfect and good. Every phase of the word light, from the original light in the natural world to the spiritual glory of the celestial, is found in The Holy Bible. God represents them all–natural light (the light of day), artificial light (temporary substitute), miraculous light (supernatural), mental, moral, and spiritual light (inner life of man). Thus, our fellowship with one another should encompass all of the light that represents our Heavenly Father.

22

3.

The Illumination of Light

The illumination of light makes things clear.   The light of the body is the eye. If the eye is clear then the whole body shall be full of light. As your light illuminates, you offer clarity unto others.

(Matthew 6:22)

"Then Jesus said unto them, 'Yet a little while is the light with you. Walk while ye have the light, lest darkness come upon you: for he that walketh in darkness knoweth not whither he goeth.'"

(John 12:35)

During the triumphal entry of Jesus Christ, Andrew and Philip learn a valuable lesson–teach others as I have taught you. Illuminate the ways for others so that they will not stumble in spiritual darkness.

"I am come a light into the world, that whosoever believeth on me should not abide in darkness."

(John 12:46)

Jesus cried as He teaches us to trust in God, not man.
He came to save the world on assignment
by the Heavenly Father.   The Word is life and His light
pierces the darkness of this world.
Spiritual transformation, through Jesus Christ,
is nothing to be ashamed of.

"Truly the light is sweet, and a pleasant thing it is for the eyes to behold the sun."

(Ecclesiastes 11:7)

Vanity – the futile emptiness of trying to be happy apart from God – appears 37 times. It is intended to express the very things that cannot be understood about life.
Eccelesiastes – 'preacher' – is the autobiography of Solomon. He recognizes, and regrets, his folly and wasted time due to carnality and idolatry.   Enjoyment of life is fulfilled in the light of the Lord. It is sweet and pleasant.

"Again, a new commandment I write unto you,
which thing is true in Him and in you: because
the darkness is past, and the true light now shineth."

(1 John 2:8)

Jesus Christ, the true light, is ever shining in our hearts.
Make God visible through your good works, lifestyle,
and joy that is in your heart.

"For the commandment is a lamp; and the law is light; and reproofs of instruction are the way of life."

(Proverbs 6:23)

The illumination of God's word is revealed in this Scripture. Illumination is that divine process whereby God causes the written revelation to be understood by the human heart. Prior to illumination is revelation and inspiration. Reveal God's Word to the lost and inspire them to walk in the newness of life.

"But the path of the just is as the shining light, that shineth more and more unto the perfect day."

(Proverbs 4:18)

You light the way for those who walk in the path of the wicked. Never let your light dwindle because others depend upon you more than you know.

"But all things that are reproved are made manifest by the light: for whatsoever doth make manifest is light."

(Ephesians 5:13)

All sins that are exposed are made visible by the gospel, for whatever sin is made visible becomes light. Therefore, walk as children of light, exposing the unfruitful works of darkness.

"For with thee is the fountain of life: in thy light shall we see light."

(Psalm 36:9)

In this song of worship, the excellence and loving kindness of God is revealed through His light. The love for our neighbor should be as strong as God's love for us!

"And to rule over the day and over the night, to divide the light from the darkness: and God saw that it was good."

(Genesis 1:18)

God said that the light was good (verse 4). God said that it was good to divide the light from the dark. He said no such thing about the dark.

"Blessed is the people that know the joyful sound: they shall walk, O LORD, in the light of thy countenance."

(Psalm 89:15)

In the midst of affliction, you are blessed. Walk in the light with joy. Never allow your countenance to discourage others. With God on your side, nothing can harm you. .

4.

The Radiance of Light

God's Word is always present
in your life. It continually radiates
as a lamp unto your feet and
a light unto your path.

(Psalm 119:105)

"And there shall be no night there; and they need no
candle, neither light of the sun; for the Lord God
giveth them light: and they shall reign
forever and ever."

(Revelation 22:5)

Light and dark will not co-exist in heaven. Walk in the
light now as you will in heaven to show all that Jesus
is the truth, the way, and the life.

"Giving thanks unto the Father, which hath made us
meet to be partakers of the inheritance
of the saints in light."

(Colossians 1:12)

God's will is that you accept, trust, obey, and respond
to His Word.   Spiritual transformation made you able
to receive an inheritance–covenant rights and benefits.
Live according to His Word and inspire others
to do the same.

"But ye are a chosen generation, a royal priesthood,
a holy nation, a peculiar people; that ye should shew
forth the praises of Him who hath called you out
of darkness into His marvelous light."

(1 Peter 2:9)

Darkness no longer reigns within you.
You have been called out.   Praise Him for
His excellence and let His light radiate from the crown
of your head to the soles of your feet.

"He revealeth the deep and secret things:
He knoweth what is in the darkness, and the light
dwelleth with Him."

(Daniel 2:22)

Daniel openly acknowledged his God before King
Nebuchadnezzar.   Because of Daniel's reputation and
boldness, he let it be known that God's light dwells
within him. Nebuchadnezzar made a decree that
no one could speak against Daniel's God.

38

"In whom the god of this world hath blinded the minds of them which believe not, lest the light of the glorious gospel of Christ, who is the image of God, should shine unto them."

(2 Corinthians 4:4)

—⟨◦⟩—

You are to make God clear and visible.
As an ambassador for Christ, you are to be visible.
Allow your light to radiate as a means to give hope
to those who have lost hope. Do not hide.

"And He shall bring forth thy righteousness
as the light, and thy judgment as the noonday.

(Psalm 37:6)

As light dispels darkness, righteousness dispels
unrighteousness. Your light is meant to penetrate, expose,
and reveal. Good wins over evil every time!

"The sun shall be no more thy light by day; neither for brightness shall the moon give light unto thee: but the LORD shall be unto thee an everlasting light, and thy God thy glory. Thy sun shall no more go down; neither shall thy moon withdraw itself: for the LORD shall be thine everlasting light, and the days of thy mourning shall be ended."

(Isaiah 60:19-20)

God is an everlasting light that never dwindles or diminishes. It is the true light that resides inside of the believer.   It radiates as brightly on the inside of you. Look only to God for clear directions for your life.

41

O house of Jacob, come ye, and let us walk in the light of the LORD.

(Isaiah 2:5)

Your path and future is bright.   That path has already been lit by your Heavenly Father.
Walk with the Lord.

5.

Expose and Expel Darkness

Dark is the opposite of Light. God divided the light and called it good. He said no such thing about the darkness.

(Genesis 1:4 & 18)

"For God, who commanded the light to shine
out of darkness, hath shined in our hearts, to give
the light of the knowledge of the glory of God
in the face of Jesus Christ."

(2 Corinthians 4:6)

Light promotes growth and productivity.   Your desire
to know God's word is planted in your heart.
As His light permeates throughout your body,
the knowledge of Him becomes more and more clear.
Seek to know Him!

"And God said, 'Let there be light: and there was light.'"

(Genesis 1:3)

God's first recorded words!
Light brought organization to chaos.
Then, God said it was good.

"Therefore judge nothing before the time,
until the Lord come, who both will bring to light
the hidden things of darkness, and will make manifest
the counsels of the hearts: and then shall every man
have praise of God."

(1 Corinthians 4:5)

What is done in the dark shall ultimately be revealed
in the light.

"Ye are all the children of light, and the children of the day: we are not of the night, nor of darkness."

(1 Thessalonians 5:5)

Day and night are opposites, as are light and darkness. Therefore, your light has a purpose–to show others the way and to encourage them to live according to God's principles. Spread the gospel–repel darkness.

"Unto the upright there ariseth light in the darkness: he is gracious, and full of compassion, and righteous."

(Psalm 112:4)

The blessings of those who fear God are awesome. This Psalm (verses 1 –10) admonishes you to fear God and to enjoy your blessings. The wicked shall see it, and be grieved, shall gnash their teeth, and melt away. Their desire to be wicked shall perish (verse 10).

"Then Jesus said unto them, 'Yet a little while is the light with you. Walk while ye have the light, lest darkness come upon you: for he that walketh in darkness knoweth not whither he goeth.'"

(John 12:35)

Jesus, our masterful Teacher, warns that to walk in darkness will result in not knowing where you are going. Walk in the light as if the lives of others depends upon it. Seek and save the lost through your light.

Contact Kevin Wayne Johnson at
Writing for the Lord Ministries
Clarksville, Maryland www.writingforthelord.com
kevin@writingforthelord.com

Other books by Kevin Wayne Johnson:

Give God the Glory! Called to be Light in the Workplace
Give God the Glory! Know God and Do the Will of God
Concerning Your Life